FAR

A Guffer's Guide

FARTING

A Guffer's Guide

I. Dunwun

First published in Great Britain in 2005 by
Michael O'Mara Books Limited
9 Lion Yard
Tremadoc Road
London SW4 7NQ

A CIP catalogue record for this book is available from the British Library

ISBN 1-84317-165-1

www.mombooks.com

Cover design by Glen Saville
Designed and typeset by Design 23

Printed in Great Britain by William Clowes Ltd., Beccles, Suffolk

CONTENTS

INTRODUCTION

The study of farting, which I like to term Guffology, is something that has fascinated man for millennia. The philosopher and physician Hippocrates warned of the dangers of holding in your farts (see page 64), so clearly they were as troubled in ancient times as we are today. Not that everyone views farting as a problem; there are many who revel in the joys of flatulence, savouring each pungent whiff, every tuneful trumpet. For most of us, however, while the sound and scent of our own parps are perfectly acceptable – perhaps even pleasantly relaxing when there has been a build-up of tension prior to the blow-off – other people's whumps remain fundamentally offensive. One of the main aims of Guffologists everywhere is to find a way of imbuing the belligerent bottom blasts with an odour, if not a sound, that will make frequent farting more socially acceptable.

If a fart, for example, could be produced that manifested itself with the tinkling of wind chimes and the aroma of honeysuckle or a summer rose garden, ladies especially would feel more comfortable about dropping one in company. Letting off would suddenly become a far more acceptable thing to do. Women sitting in the hairdressers would compliment each other on the quality of their guffs and chat about what they had eaten, drunk or shoved up their backsides to produce such a melodious and daintily perfumed parp. Perfume manufacturers might be able to introduce whole new product lines for use in places that perfumes have not previously been squirted. And the family dog would no longer have to suffer the disgrace of being sent from the room, bearing the brunt of the blame for a stinker he never emitted.

If farts could be perfumed, of course, gentlemen would be able to produce manly odours to be admired – the round, sweet scent of port for an after-dinner parp or, for drinking beer at the bar, hoppy guffs that pop out in a series of delightful cracks like a donkey walking over bubble wrap. Of course, if such control could be exerted, then it is entirely feasible that we might be able to introduce into the fart an aphrodisiac quality and I might get laid at last ... every night ... several times.

Being able to control the fart would also have an effect on the crime rate throughout the nation. My country house at Little Clench, near Pratt's Bottom, invariably must stand with most of the windows wide open. This is a clear invitation to thieves and I have been burgled many times, although the intruders have never lingered long enough actually to steal anything. In fact, the last burglar broke in and left a vase of flowers and a can of air freshener on the table.

Guffology, then, may one day change our lives for ever, but in the meantime we must content ourselves with learning all there is to know about the fart, in order that we can better understand the causes and effects of this enchanting phenomenon.

I. Evan Dunwun, 2005

WHY DO WE FART?

Why do we fart? The answer to that question is not, of course, that it feels fantastic, makes your mates laugh or clears the family out of the room so that you can flip the TV channel over to the football. These are all sound reasons for farting, but they do not actually explain why farts happen. So what exactly is a fart? For a start, a fart is nothing to be ashamed of. It is the most perfectly natural thing in the world. Farting is, in fact, essential to life.

The simple, honest fart is one way in which nature expels certain toxins from our bodies. Flatulence is caused by a build up of gas in the stomach or intestines. If we didn't fart, the gases we produce while processing food and drink would be re-absorbed into our bloodstreams and poison us. When you really need to fart, of course, you can feel the pressure building and that increasing pressure can cause extreme discomfort if not released, as anyone who has suffered from trapped wind can tell you.

If you were so prudish as simply to refuse ever to fart, it is unlikely that gas would simply go on accumulating inside you until you swelled up like a barrage balloon. That which was not absorbed into your blood would find a way out somehow, but I suspect that some victims of that peculiar phenomenon 'spontaneous human combustion' might not have gone up in flames if only they had learned how to enjoy a good guff.

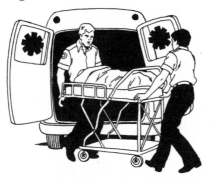

Another case of spontaneous human combustion that could have been avoided with a good fart.

WHAT ARE LITTLE FARTS MADE OF?

Well it's not sugar and spice and all things nice, that's for sure. The gases that go to make up the average fart are a combination of those found in the air that we breathe and those produced when matter starts to decay or, in this case, is broken down (digested) by the acid and bacteria in our stomachs. The main gases found in a fart cloud are as follows:

Nitrogen	N_2
Oxygen	O_2
Carbon Dioxide	CO_2
Hydrogen	H_2
Methane	CH_4

Farts can have a surprisingly complex chemical composition

That nitrogen and oxygen are present in your farts should come as no surprise. Most of the air that we breathe in is composed of nitrogen and oxygen is, of course, what we most need to extract from that air. The others, however, are highly dangerous, so let's take a closer look at that stuff that comes trumpeting out of your backside.

NITROGEN

Nitrogen forms approximately 78 per cent of the air that we breathe, so it's all around us as well as inside us. Given that we are in contact with it every second of every day of our lives, it's pretty clear that nitrogen does us no particular harm. It is also a colourless, odourless gas and produces no major reactions, if you discount that strange squint in your eye when it comes whistling through your ringpiece.

Nitrogen does, however, help in the formation of indole and skatole, compounds that are created during the putrefaction of food and the production of faecal matter. That's how it gets in to your farts.

OXYGEN

Considering that oxygen is essential for keeping us alive, it maintains a fairly low profile among the big boys of the gas world. It has no colour, it has no smell, it has no taste, yet it is one of the most common elements in the earth's crust and it is highly reactive. Nothing, in fact, will burn without oxygen. Starve a fire of oxygen by smothering it with a blanket or with sand and it will go out. Fan a fire with extra oxygen, like a blacksmith would with his bellows, and it will burn more fiercely. Remember that when you drop one in front of the barbecue.

CARBON DIOXIDE

Most people know that this gas is the main constituent of the 'used' air that we breathe out of our mouths and noses. It's not so commonly known that we also emit it from the other end. A little over half the gas content of a fart will be composed of CO_2.

When dissolved in water, CO_2 forms carbonic acid, the stuff that gives fizzy drinks their pop, so it's guaranteed to make for a lively fart, but CO_2 is also the gas used in fire extinguishers as it smothers flames. In a room full of CO_2, you would also be smothered, but it's good to know that it's there, especially when you consider how dangerous two of the other main fart gases can be.

HYDROGEN

Hydrogen is the lightest and most abundant element in the universe. It combines with oxygen in H_2O to make water, something without which none of us can survive long, but it also has a far more sinister side to its nature. Hydrogen is highly flammable, but because it is lighter than air it was used to fill the giant pre-WWII German airships, resulting in tragedy when the *Hindenburg* caught fire while docking at Lakehurst, New Jersey, after an Atlantic crossing from Frankfurt. There were over ninety people on board and thirty-six lost their lives.

Hydrogen is also used to make atomic bombs, so what chance have your pants got really?

It stinks when combined with sulphur to form hydrogen sulphide (H_2S).

METHANE

Methane produces the fart of the devil. Also known as marsh gas because it is released by rotting vegetation in swamps and on river beds, methane is produced during the decomposition of organic matter – pretty much everything you eat, in other words.

The layers of decayed vegetation which, over the millennia, have formed underground layers of carbon that is mined as coal, contain pockets of trapped gas – mainly methane. When miners blundered into these pockets in days gone by, before they could say, 'Who's dropped one?', the candles of their lamps would ignite the methane and blow them all to bits. Methane burns with a violent blue or green flame tempting some tricksters to set light to their farts for a display of anal pyrotechnics. They are risking the loss not only of their pubic hair but all that it keeps cosy.

Other Things In Your Farts

The five main gases in the average whump will combine with products of other things you might have eaten to create marvellous concoctions that are best cleared out of your intestines. Unfortunately, anyone you happen to be in conversation with when these substances evacuate your bowels may feel the need to evacuate the room. These are the real pong-whiffy stinkers.

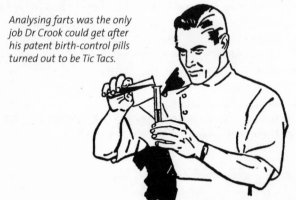

Analysing farts was the only job Dr Crook could get after his patent birth-control pills turned out to be Tic Tacs.

METHYL-INDOLE

When methane combines with indole produced by decomposing proteins it produces methyl-indole, a gas that smells so bad that one whiff shocks people into the sort of wide-eyed expression that leaves their contact lenses lying lost on the carpet.

SKATOLE

This delightful gas is formed from carbon, hydrogen and nitrogen and takes its name from the Greek word *skatos*, meaning dung. Despite the smell making you feel like you're wearing a horse's arse for a hat, skatole, like methyl-indole, is actually used in making perfume!

HYDROGEN SULPHIDE

It's colourless and poisonous, it burns and it's not called 'rotten-egg gas' for nothing.

THINGS THAT MAKE YOU GO PARP

Everyone knows, through a process of trial and error, which foods are most likely to make them let rip. Once they are aware of those things which have a particularly flatulent effect, some choose to avoid such foods. They are not only missing out on some of the most delicious of delicacies, but also on the delights of a fulsome fluff.

It is a matter of record that vegetarians fart more than carnivores. Hitler, a confirmed vegetarian, was also a gargantuan guffer, although there is no truth in the rumour that the explosion which almost blew him to bits during one of the many attempts to assassinate him was actually no more than one of his own backfires.

Vegetables are more difficult to digest than most types of meat and produce exactly the kinds of gases required for a deeply satisfying fart. The roughage in a vegetarian's diet also helps to promote healthy bowel movements, so eat your greens if you want to parp on a higher plane.

APRICOTS
Historically renowned for giving sailors the runs.

BEANS
Practically any type of bean is good for farting, but baked beans are famous for it and curried baked beans produce almost instantaneous results.

BEER
Gassy beers are obviously good for adding immediate volume to stomach gases (try not to burp it all away) but a good, hoppy real ale can also have spectacular effects.

BRAN
Excellent for starting the day on a high note.

BRUSSELS SPROUTS
A Christmas party farty favourite. Stock up fresh when they are in season and freeze for use throughout the year. Brilliant fart inducers when used along with any kind of pulses for a Boxing Day soup.

CABBAGE

Like a big sprout, but its size does dilute the effect slightly. However, sauerkraut, made with fermented cabbage, keeps it right up there on the farting leader board.

CHEWING GUM

Even if you don't swallow the gum, you swallow enough air while chewing it to fill a bouncy castle, and all those chemicals brew up nicely.

CHILLI

Positively the best way to engender a lively afterburner, but also believed by some to be good for asthma, arthritis, blood clots and shingles.

CURRY

If you don't fart after a good, hot curry, then it's probably already killed you. Curries are also thought to help induce childbirth, but only in women.

You can love beans too much.

Eggs
Contain sulphur so they give you sinfully stinky farts.

Figs
Renowned for their ability to get you going.

Garlic
The unique property of garlic is that it can make you stink at both ends.

Haggis
There's a reason why it's windy in the glens.

Leeks
Good, healthy fibrous vegetables that make a truly dangerous soup when mixed with lentils or split peas.

Lentils
Like all types of pulses, lentils evolve into violent fart gas almost before you've finished your meal.

MILK
Comes out of a cow and they are master farters, so it's got to do some good.

NUTS
Various effects can be achieved using nuts, but stories of energetic farters producing a gas-powered anal peanut machine gun are surely apocryphal.

ONIONS
Like leeks, onions, either raw in salads or cooked, especially in a dopiaza curry, produce sure-fire farts.

PEAS
Almost any kind of peas from chick to mushy will produce a pleasing parp.

PICKLES
What better way to enhance the flatulence-inducing qualities of any vegetable than to pickle it?

Plums
Like prunes, plums and most other soft fruits give off fantastic guffing gases as the bacteria break them down.

Radishes
Produce a peppery, piquant, pungent parp.

Spices
Spices are good for stimulating the gut and cleaning out your system, so they often bring with them not only their own aroma, but some that may have been lurking inside for quite a while.

Steak
In a pepper sauce, with onions or just slapped on the barbecue, a big steak will fill you up, causing plenty of activity for a lively, hot fart.

Watercress
Can produce surprisingly large results for a bit of greenery that looks so insignificant.

WORDS OF WISDOM

Winds at night are always bright;
But winds in the morning, sailors take warning.
Weather lore

PARPING POETRY –
SIMPLY HEAVENLY

An angel strumming her harp
Let loose an almighty parp
'Good God,' said St Peter,
As he went out to greet her,
'Was that an A flat or B sharp?'

FARTING RECIPES

There are few things more invigorating than a wholesome meal that brews up a volley of thunderous farts and sets your motions in motion. The recipes on these pages can be knocked up in no time and once the meal is consumed, savoured for days afterwards. They require only the most basic of ingredients and implements but preparation is the key, so use the following as a checklist before you embark on these culinary delights.

YOU WILL NEED:

A blender, food processor
  or hand whisk
Sharp knife
Potato masher
Large bowl
A medium-sized saucepan
An omelette pan
Deep-fat fryer

BASIC INGREDIENTS:

Garlic powder
Curry powder
Chilli powder
Tinned baked beans
Dried chillies
Dried apricots
Eggs
Canned beer
White bread
Spam

The almost immediate effect of curried sprouts is a real ice-breaker at dinner parties.

SPROUT CURRY

Sprouts are one of the best foodstuffs any confirmed farter can consume for enhanced performance of both volume and aroma. Once eaten, keep an air freshener handy for a couple of days.

INGREDIENTS:

1.5 kilos fresh, green Brussels sprouts (washed and outer leaves removed)

250 fl oz water

1/2 x 5ml spoon salt

1/4 x 5ml ground ginger

25g butter

1 onion, peeled and finely chopped

2 1/2 x 5ml curry powder

1/2 x 5ml ground coriander

1. Using a sharp knife, make a small cross in the base of each sprout and place in a large saucepan. Cover with cold, salted water. Leave to soak for 30 minutes. Drain and place in 250 fl oz cold water and ½ teaspoon of salt. Bring to the boil, then simmer for 15 minutes or until soft. Drain and mash to a pulp using a potato masher.

2. Melt the butter in a large frying pan. Add the onion and cook until transparent but not brown.

3. Add the mashed sprouts to the frying pan and stir over a low heat until they are heated through.

4. Stir in the curry powder, ground coriander and ginger and cook for a further 15 minutes.

5. Serve piping hot as an accompaniment to Deep-Fried Scotch Eggs or on its own as a vegetarian snack.

SERVES 4

DEEP-FRIED SCOTCH EGGS

A perennial favourite north of the border where the population are enthusiastic deep-fryers and will pop anything from the famous Mars Bar to pizzas, sausages, and just about anything else that's not fit enough to run away, into a vat of hot fat. The results are usually powerful enough to make your kilt swirl.

INGREDIENTS:
1/2 kg pork sausage meat
1 small onion, peeled and finely chopped
1 x 5ml tsp each of finely chopped fresh parsley, sage, mint and rosemary
4 eggs, hard-boiled and shelled
Flour for coating
1 egg, beaten
Approx 175g dried breadcrumbs
Oil for deep frying

1. Put the sausage meat, onion and mixed herbs together in a bowl and mix well.

2. Divide the mixture into four and press firmly around the hard-boiled eggs.

3. Roll in flour then dip in beaten egg.

4. Coat evenly with breadcrumbs. Chill in refrigerator for at least 1 hour before frying.

5. Heat the oil gently in a deep-fat fryer until it is hot enough to turn a stale bread cube golden in about 20-30 seconds (180°-190°C / 350°-370°F on a deep-fat frying thermometer). Fry the Scotch eggs two at a time for about 10 minutes until they are crisp and golden-brown.

6. Drain on absorbent kitchen paper and keep warm while frying the remaining two Scotch eggs. Drain, transfer to a hot serving platter and serve. Alternatively serve cold as a snack with crisp green salad.

CHILLI BUTTY

If all the beer you drank with it left you too bagged out to finish all of that giant pot of chilli you made, this is a great way to use up leftovers. It's also a great way to eat chilli if you simply can't be bothered messing around with all that fiddly rice.

INGREDIENTS:

Cooking oil for frying
1 large onion, peeled and sliced
1 garlic clove, crushed with 1 x 2.5ml salt
3/4 kg minced beef
1 x 5ml chilli powder (or more if you're brave)
1 x 396g can tomatoes
150 ml beef stock
1 x 5ml spoon sugar
2 x 15 ml spoons tomato purée
Freshly ground black pepper

1 x 432g can red kidney beans, drained and
rinsed in cold running water
Sliced white bread
Butter

1. Heat 2 tablespoons of oil in a large pan. Add the onion
and garlic and fry gently until golden.

2. Add the beef and chilli powder and fry until the meat is
well browned, stirring constantly.

3. Stir in the tomatoes, stock, sugar, tomato purée and
pepper to taste and bring to the boil. Lower the heat, cover
and simmer gently for 30 minutes, adding the drained
kidney beans 5 minutes before the end of the cooking
time.

4. Adjust seasoning and serve immediately between two
slices of buttered bread.

TWELVE-EGG OMELETTE WITH BEER

Eggs are fantastic value when it comes to farts, providing a sulphurous whiff that can clear a room faster than you can say, 'For God's sake, open the window!' Combine them with some fine canned beer and those annoying neighbours might finally be persuaded to keep their noses out of your business.

INGREDIENTS:

12 eggs, beaten
Salt and freshly ground
black pepper
½ pint best bitter
2 tablespoons oil

'If he guffs one more time, this is going over his head.'

34

1. Beat the beer into the beaten egg until foaming and frothy (the mixture that is, not you).

2. Add salt and pepper to taste.

3. Heat the oil in a very large frying pan and pour in the mixture.

4. Cook for 5 minutes until the mixture has set then turn and cook for 5 minutes on the other side. Alternatively, if turning the set mix looks like it's going to be a problem, you can stick the whole pan under a hot grill to do the top.

5. Slide the omelette out of the pan onto a large plate and serve slices of it with a crisp green salad.

SPICY MANGO SURPRISE

Mangoes make an excellent dessert, and fruit on the whole is a pleasant, if anti-climactic way to round off a meal. The surprise is that this fruit dessert supplies no respite whatsoever from the onslaught of fart fodder you have previously consumed, because it is laced with chilli powder. The cream will help to calm things down a bit if you are feeling too shell-shocked.

INGREDIENTS:

3 mangoes
5 teaspoons icing sugar
1 teaspoon chilli powder
Enough double cream to relieve the flatulently exhausted

1. Slice the mangoes in half, avoiding the flattish stone inside.

2. Make deep criss-cross slashes through the flesh of each half mango but not all the way through the skin, creating a grid of roughly 1/2-inch (1-cm) squares.

3. When each half has been cut, you should be able to turn each one inside out, like a hedgehog.

4. Combine the chilli powder and icing sugar then sprinkle onto each mango half.

5. Grill for 5-10 minutes under a medium heat until the icing sugar starts to caramelize.

6. Serve with double cream

You just know who'll get the blame . . .

FIZZY LEMON SHERBET SORBET

If, after all that guff-inducing fare, you feel you need something to cool down your insides without spoiling the effect you anticipate tomorrow, this little sorbet is just the job, supplying enough fizz to keep that parp gas popping.

INGREDIENTS;
4 oz (100g) granulated sugar
4 fl oz (100ml) water
Zest, juice and pulp of 2 lemons
3 fl oz (75ml) orange juice
Packet of sherbet

1. Dissolve the sugar in the water in a saucepan.

2. Bring to the boil and then simmer for 10 minutes to make a syrup.

3. Allow to cool fully and mix in the zest, juice and pulp of the lemons and the orange juice.

4. Put the mixture in a suitable container, cover and freeze until slushy, for about 1 hour.

5. Transfer the mixture to a food processor with a metal blade and process until smooth, or stir vigorously with a metal spoon.

6. Put back into the container, cover and freeze for a further hour.

7. Stir briefly, fold in the sherbet and freeze for another hour.

8. Serve garnished with curls of lemon peel.

WORDS OF WISDOM

All citizens shall be allowed to pass gas
whenever necessary.
CLAUDIUS CAESAR

FARTING ALL OVER THE WORLD

Those who travel around the globe will, from time to time, have the opportunity to partake of the delights of foreign food and may well be taken by surprise by the effects it can have. If you have tried to squeeze out a discreet silent one while sitting at a pavement café, think you've got away with it but need to check if anyone around you has noticed the aroma, here are some key fart words to listen out for.

LANGUAGE	FARTWORD
Afrikaans	*poep*
Albanian	*mfryet*
Arabic	*eeyagas*
Cantonese	*fong*

Danish	*fis*
Finnish	*pieru*
French	*pet*
Gaelic	*braim*
German	*Furz*
Greek	*perdomai*
Hawaiian	*pu'u puhi'u foully*
Hungarian	*koz*
Italian	*peto*
Japanese	*hohi*

Latin	*peditum*
Norwegian	*fis*
Polish	*pierdzenic*
Portugese	*peido*
Spanish	*pedo*
Swedish	*fjärt*
Thai	*tod*
Welsh	*gwynt*

USEFUL FOREIGN PHRASES

FRENCH

Où sont les toilettes? Je ne me sens pas bien.
Where is the toilet? I don't feel well.

Papier toilette!
Toilet paper!

Faut-il changer le combination pour le dîner?
Do I have to put on a new spacesuit for dinner?

Je n'arrive pas à ouvrir les fenêtres.
I can't get these windows open.

Ça sent pas la rose!
It stinks (literally, it doesn't smell like a rose).

SWEDISH

Var vänlig visa mig till avdelningen för pruttkuddar.
Please point me to the whoopee-cushion department.

Er hund har visst fisit igen.
Your dog seems to have farted again.

Är det mycket vitlök I den här grytan?
Does this stew contain a lot of garlic?

Man ska vädra sin åsikter.
One should give air to one's opinions.

¡Quiero comer las judias por las cena!
I want to have beans for supper!

¡Me encanta el fiabre enlatado hecho con carne de cerdo!
I love spam!

¿Donde esta los servicios?
Where is the loo?

No hay mas papel higiéncico.
There is no loo paper left.

¿Tienes una mascara?
Do you have a mask?

¡Ten cuidado, me perro va a eliminar gases!
Be careful, my dog is about to break wind.

AFRIKAANS

Waar kan ek 'n kerrie ëet?
Where can I get a good curry?

Ek wil boentjies vir aandete he.
I want beans for supper.

Ek het te veel blomkool geëet.
I've eaten too much cabbage.

Dit luik sleg!
That smells terrible!

Questa birra tedesca me fa scureggiare come una tromba!
This German beer is making me fart like a trumpet!

Lui ha appena fatto una puzza della madonna!
He's just done a really smelly one!

Le Tre Scuregge (The 3 Farts)

1. *Siquam: silenziosa quasi mortale*
   Silent but deadly

2. *Tadem: tanfo della Madonna*
   A really smelly one

3. *Bosef: boata senza fetore*
   A thunderfart.

Che puzza!
What a stink!

POLISH

Ten gulasz jest ostry!
This goulash is spicy!

Ta zupa z kapusty jest dobra.
This cabbage soup is good.

Chcialabym jajko na sniadanie.
I would like four eggs for breakfast.

Smierdzi okropnie w tym pokoju.
It smells bad in this room.

'*Smierdzi okropnie
w tym pokoju.*'

49

SOUNDS OMINOUS

Only the most proficient of farters who have practised long and hard can ever boast enough sphincter control to be able to guff discreetly, letting out a silent one that can be ignored or, when it makes its presence smelt, blamed on someone else. For novices there is no way to guarantee that letting one go, however carefully, will not come out like a creaking gate or a clap of thunder. Most farts, therefore, will be accompanied by a tell-tale trumpeting but describing the exact sound has always been something of a problem for writers.

Douglas Adams and John Lloyd in *The Meaning of Liff* described the sound of a rather mediocre, unsatisfying fart as 'Pfpt'. You can imagine the hissing noise they were driving at, but representing it in this way is almost as disappointing as the event itself. In *Grossology*, a children's book

Will I ever get that fart sound right?

about distasteful things, Sylvia Branzei tried 'flub, flubba, fwwp, which might have a hugely significant meaning for the Flowerpot Men but doesn't really capture the distinct tone she was looking for that accompanies a rather limp, half-hearted effort. Sylvia also experimented with 'fwwt', 'put-put-put', 'pwwwbbb' and 'flubba-flub' with no greater success. Even immensely respected writers like James Joyce have struggled a bit with the fart sound. In *Ulysses*, Joyce went for 'Karaaaaaaa . . . Pprrpffrrppffff,' which is a good enough stab at it to make you not want to be sitting beside him in a curry house, but still doesn't really encapsulate the sound of a truly great fart.

What most writers have failed to grasp is that all of the words that are used to describe the noble bottom blast have been carefully crafted in an onomatopoeic way that makes them the most accurate representations of the sound of the dastardly deed. Fart, parp, guff, squeak, fluff, burp, hiss, rip, braft, rift, fritty, trat, trump, rax, toot, whiff, honk, bark, belch, blurt and whump are all good, honest farting words that both say and sound like what they mean. The difference between these and something like 'fwwt' or 'pfpt' is that the latter sound like some kind of small-denomination East European currency. You could easily imagine buying a beer in a Bulgarian bar and being given sixteen fwwt in your change, but no one's ever going to pass a 'whump' over the counter. The answer, then, is simple – there are

Of course! You need vowels in your bowels!

vowels in your bowels. A, E, I, O or U should always be used when describing precisely the sound effect achieved when a fellow farter has just dropped one. Consonants just can't hack it on their own. Aspiring authors take note.

PARPING POETRY –
ON THE GOOD SHIP *VENUS*

The first mate's name was Carter,
My God, he was a farter.
When the wind wouldn't blow
And the ship wouldn't go,
They used Carter the farter to start 'er.

'Friggin' In The Riggin', traditional

FARTING IN LITERATURE

Since people have been farting from long before we learned to walk upright (probably to get away from the smell) it should come as no surprise that people have been writing about farts ever since man first put reed pen to papyrus. The most famous farts in English literature are probably those in 'The Miller's Tale' from Geoffrey Chaucer's *The Canterbury Tales* but he also managed to slip in an entire story based around farting in 'The Summoner's Tale'.

The plot concerns a greedy friar who is desperate to claim a legacy from a dying man, an inheritance to be shared equally among the twelve members of his order. The Summoner, angry at the friar's avarice, decides to take his revenge. He tells the friar to reach behind the man to find his legacy, but as the friar fumbles around the dying man's backside, he is rewarded with an almighty guff. Having vowed to share the inheritance equally among his brethren, he then has to find a way to distribute equally the sound and smell of the parp.

The Canterbury Tales dates from the fourteenth century, but Chaucer was neither the first nor the only man of literature to write about farting. Guffing abounds in the works of Robert Burns, James Joyce, Henry Fielding, Daniel Defoe, J. P. Donleavy, John Skelton, Henry Miller, John Wilmot (Earl of Rochester), Charles Sackville (Lord Buckhurst), George Villiers (Duke of Buckingham) and many, many others. Like all storytellers, they recognized that the common man likes nothing better than to read about the commonest of things. The fact that you are doing it now proves the point.

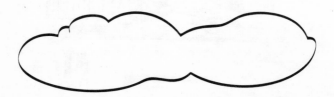

In *A Reed Shaken By The Wind*, Gavin Maxwell writes of his journey among the marsh Arabs of Iraq and recounts an ancient traditional tale told to him in a remote region of the country. A young man farted at the Court of the Persian king and immediately exiled himself in disgrace to a far-off land. When he returned, old and grey, he was stopped at the frontier by a border guard who asked him how long ago he had left the country. When the old man told him the year, the guard said, 'Ah, yes, that was the year some bloke farted at Court.'

A similar tale is told by the English antiquary and biographer John Aubrey (1626-1697) in his *Brief Lives*, where he describes the embarrassment felt by the court poet Edward de Vere, seventeenth Earl of Oxford (1550-1604), who dropped an involuntary fart in the presence of Queen Elizabeth I:

'Your Majesty . . . whoops! I'd better go travelling . . .'

This Earl of Oxford, making of his low
obeisance to Queen Elizabeth, happened to
let a Fart, at which he was so abashed and
ashamed that he went on to travel, 7 years.
On his return the Queen welcomed him home
and said, 'My Lord, I has forgot the Fart.'

Edward Lear (1812-1888), the English artist, traveller and
writer best known for his children's books, especially his
A Book of Nonsense and its successors, wrote
affectionately of a favourite farting duchess who gave
enormous dinner parties attended by the cream of
society. One night she gave off a gargantuan guff, a real
conversation stopper, that simply could not be allowed
to pass without comment. Thinking fast, she glowered at
her butler and snapped, 'Hawkins – stop that!'
'Certainly, Your Grace,' replied the butler. 'Which way did
it go?'

The French novelist Honoré de Balzac (1799-1850), author of the great collection of novels under the general title *La Comédie humaine* which includes *Eugénie Grandet, Le Père Goriot* and *La Cousine Bette,* is said to have remarked, 'I should like one of these days to be so well known, so popular, so celebrated, so famous, that it would permit me . . . to break wind in society, and society would think it a most natural thing.' Unfortunately for him, the vulgarity in his work, and in his own general behaviour, often had exactly the opposite effect, scandalizing members of the literary establishment.

Sir John Suckling (1609-1642) was a poet and one of the leading lights in the Royalist movement in the early days of King Charles I's conflict with Parliament. He is described by *The Oxford Companion To English Literature* as 'one of the most elegant of the Cavalier poets'. His take on fluffing was expressed in his poem 'Love's Offence':

> Love is the fart
> Of every heart,
> It pains a man when kept close,
> And others doth offend, when 'tis let loose.

The best way to illustrate the huge importance of guffing in great literature is to give a few examples, so here are some immortal lines from writers who would all have agreed that the pen is mightier than the sword, but that neither will protect you from a vicious afterburner.

A man may break a word with you, sir; and words are but the wind; Ay; and break it in your face, so he break it not behind.
WILLIAM SHAKESPEARE, *The Comedy of Errors*

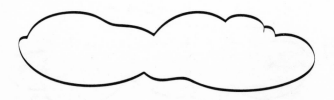

What winde can there blowe,
That doth not some man please?
A fart in the blowying
Doth the blower ease.
JOHN HEYWOOD (1497–1580)

Who has seen the wind?
Neither you nor I:
But when the trees bow down their heads,
The wind is passing by.
CHRISTINA ROSSETTI, 'Who Has Seen The Wind?'

Not I, not I, but the wind that blows
through me!
D. H. LAWRENCE,
'Song Of A Man Who Has Come Through'

What comfort can the vortices of Descartes
give to a man who has whirlwinds in his
bowels?
BENJAMIN FRANKLIN (1706–90)

It is best for flatulence to pass without noise
and breaking, though it is better for it to pass
with noise than to be intercepted and
accumulated internally.
HIPPOCRATES, (c.460–c.357 BC)

I had forgot much ... gone with the wind ...
ERNEST DOWSON,
'Non Sum Qualis Eram'

The wind flapped loose, the wind was still,
Shaken out dead from tree and hill:
I had walked on at the wind's will, –
I sat now, for the wind was still.
DANTE GABRIEL ROSSETTI,
'The Woodspurge'

Surprised by joy – impatient as the Wind ...
WILLIAM WORDSWORTH,
'Surprised By Joy'

TOP TWENTY BESTSELLING FART BOOKS
(or would have been if they'd ever been written)

Much Ado About Guffing

Bridget Jones's Diarrhoea

Catcher in the Rear

The Secret Dump Of Adrian Mole Aged 13¾

The Da Vinci Crack Splitter

Fart of Darkness

The Guffenberg Bible

Harry Potter and the Chamber of Flatulence

Captain Correlli's Minger

Harry Potter and the Prisoner of Arsekabang

The Shipping Phews

Watered Shit Down

Parpy Clarke, Ha Ha Ha

The French Concoction

A Rear in Provence

To Gas a Mockingbird

Withering Shites

Mein Whumpf

Farter on the Orient Express

Jurassic Parp

NAME THAT FART

There are many different forms of fart and many different ways of expelling a fart, some surreptitious and some altogether more overt. There are, therefore, many different words used to describe both the act of farting and the fart itself. Anyone practising hard to become an expert farter needs to familiarize him or herself with all of the appropriate fart words.

FART WORDS – VERBS

(describing the act of farting)

Backfire
Bark
Bip
Blast
Blow Off
Blow the old bum trumpet
Break wind
Breeze
Cough
Crack a rat
Cut the cheese
Draw the mud
Drop a shoe
Drop one
Drop your guts
Fire an arseblast
Flatulate

Float an air biscuit
Fluff
Frame
Grep
Guff
Honk
Janet
Let off
Let one rip
Ming
Open your lunch box
Pass wind
Pier
Poop
Pot
Proof
Queef
Rift
Rosebud
Rumble

Shoot a bunny
Step on a duck
Totter
Trump
Woof

FART WORDS – NOUNS
(describing that which exits
your body)

Afterburner
Anal airwaves
Anal audio
Arseblast
Barking spider
Bench warmer
Bottom burp
Botty burp
Brown genie
Buck snort

Butt burner
Butt blast
Butt sneeze
Cheek flapper
Cheeser
Chuff
Crack Splitter
Disappointment
   from down under
Exploding turd
Explosion
Faecal fluffy
Firecracker
Flatulence
Gravy pants
Great brown cloud
Happy honker
Heinz burp
Hotty
I say!
Jockey's friend

Lawdy!
Mud cricket
Mud duck
Natural gas
Nature's little surprise
Nature's musical box
One gun salute
Pant stainer
Panty burp
Prelude to a shit
Pull my finger
Quaker
Raspberry tart
Tat bark
Ripper
S.A.V. – silent and violent
S.B.D. – silent but deadly
Shit siren

Shit snore
Sidewinder
Sneeze from the turtle's head
Stinker
Stinky
Thunder from down under
Tree frog
Trouser cough
Trouser ghost
Trouser ripper
Turd slamming on the brakes
Turd tootie
Under thunder
Wet one
Whump

A LETTER TO THE ROYAL ACADEMY OF BRUSSELS FROM BENJAMIN FRANKLIN

Benjamin Franklin (1706-90), the American statesman, scientist and writer, and one of the fathers of the Declaration of Independence that secured the colonies' independence from Britain, was a man of wide knowledge and an enquiring turn of mind, as this tongue-in-cheek letter from 1780 clearly shows. For although Franklin is well known for his electrical experiments using kites to attract lightning, it is wind of a different kind that concerns him here, as he offers advice that seems at times to echo the Emperor Claudius.

GENTLEMEN:

I have perus'd your late mathematical prize Question, propos'd in lieu of one in Natural Philosophy for the ensuing Year, viz: 'Une Figure quelconque donnée, on demande d'y inscrire le plus grand nombre de Fois possible une autre Figure plus petite quelconque, qui est aussi donnée.'

I was glad to find by these following words, 'L'Académie a jugé que cette Découverte, en étendant les Bornes de nos Connoissances, ne seroit pas sans Utilité,' that you esteem utility an essential point in your enquiries, which has not always been the case with all Academies; & I conclude therefore that you have given this question instead of a philosophical, or, as the learned express it, a physical one, because you could not at the Time think of a physical one that promis'd greater Utility.

Permit me then humbly to propose one of that sort for your consideration, and thro' you, if you approve it, for the serious enquiry of learned Physicians, Chemists, etc., of this enlighten'd Age.

It is universally well known, that in digesting our common Food, there is created or produced in the Bowels of human creatures, a great quantity of Wind.

That the permitting this Air to escape and mix with the Atmosphere, is usually offensive to the Company, from the fetid Smell that accompanyes it.

That all well-bred People therefore, to avoid giving

such offense, forcibly restrain the Efforts of Nature to discharge that Wind.

That so retained contrary to Nature, it not only gives frequently great present Pain, but occasions future Diseases such as habitual Cholics, Ruptures, Tympanies, &c., often destructive of the Constitution, and sometimes of Life itself.

Were it not for the odiously offensive Smell accompanying such escapes, polite People would probably be under no more Restraint in discharging such Wind in Company, than they are in spitting or in blowing their Noses.

MY PRIZE QUESTION THEREFORE SHOULD BE: To discover some Drug, wholesome and not disagreeable, to be mixed with our common Food, or Sauces, that shall render the natural discharges of Wind from our Bodies not only inoffensive, but agreeable as Perfumes.

That this is not a chimerical Project and altogether impossible, may appear from these considerations. That we already have some knowledge of the Means capable of varying that Smell. He that dines on stale Flesh, especially with much Addition of onions, shall be able to afford a stink that no company can tolerate; while he that has liv'd for some time on Vegetables only, shall have that Breath so pure as to be insensible to the most delicate Noses; and if he can manage so as to avoid the Report, he may anywhere give vent to his Griefs, unnoticed. But as there are many to whom an entire Vegetable diet would be inconvenient, and as a little quick Lime thrown into a Jakes will correct the amazing Quantity of fetid air arising from the vast Mass of putrid Matter contain'd in such Places, and render it rather pleasing to the Smell, who knows but that a little Powder of Lime (or some other thing equivalent) taken in our Food, or perhaps a Glass of lime water drank at Dinner, may have the same effect on the Air produc'd in and issuing from our Bowels? This is worth the Experiment. Certain it is also that we have the power of changing by slight means the Smell of another discharge, that of our Water. A few stems of Asparagus eaten, shall give our Urine a disagreeable Odour; and a Pill of Turpentine no bigger than a Pea, shall bestow on it the pleasing smell of violets. And why should it be thought more impossible in Nature, to find Means of making a Perfume of our Wind than of our Water?

For the Encouragement of this Enquiry (from the immortal Honour to be reasonably expected by the Inventor) let it be considered of how small Importance to Mankind, or to how small a Part of Mankind have been useful those Discoveries in Science that have heretofore made Philosophers famous. Are there twenty Men in Europe this day the happier, or even the easier for any Knowledge they have pick'd out of Aristotle? What comfort can the Vortices of Descartes give to a Man who has Whirlwinds in his Bowels! The knowledge of Newton's Mutual Attraction of the particles of matter, can it afford ease to him who is rack'd by their mutual Repulsion, and the cruel Distentions it occasions? The pleasure arising to a few Philosophers, from seeing, a few times in their Lives, the threads of Light untwisted and separated by the Newtonian Prism into seven Colours, can it be compar'd with the Ease and Comfort every Man living might feel seven times a day, by discharging freely the Wind from his Bowels? Especially if it be converted into a Perfume; for the Pleasures of one Sense being little inferior to those of another, instead of pleasing the Sight, he might delight in the Smell of those about him, and make numbers happy, which to a benevolent Mind must afford infinite Satisfaction. The generous Soul, who now endeavours to find out whether the Friends he entertains like best Claret or Burgundy, Champagne or Madeira, would then enquire also whether they choose Musk or Lilly, Rose or Bergamot, and provide accordingly. And surely such a Liberty of ex-pressing one's Scent-i-ments, & pleasing one another, is of infinitely more importance to human Happiness than that Liberty of the Press, or of abusing one another, which the English are so ready to fight and die for.

In short, this Invention, if completed, would be, as Bacon expresses it, 'Bringing philosophy home to men's Business and Bosoms'. And I cannot but conclude, that in comparison therewith for universal and continual Utility, the Science of the Philosophers aforemention'd, even with the addition, Gentlemen, of your 'figure quelconque', and the Figures inscrib'd in it, are, all together, scarcely worth a FART-HING.

LE PÉTOMANE

The first man to make a living from breaking wind in public was a French entertainer – if that's the right word – Joseph Pujol (1857-1945). His stage title was 'Le Pétomane', and his act took him from provincial fleapits to Paris, to the Moulin Rouge itself. He discovered his strange talent at an early age and first turned it into entertainment in the 1880s. His debut at the Moulin Rouge came in 1892 and was an overnight success. After all, how many people can imitate gunfire, smoke cigarettes, play tunes on a tin flute, and sound like mock bugle calls? It was said of him that Sarah Bernhardt drew box-office receipts of 8,000 francs, but Le Pétomane in a single Sunday took 20,000 francs at the box office. He could even fart the opening bars of the French national anthem.

Rarely has this usually distressing symptom been turned to such advantage. Pujol became affluent as an effluent performer, and died in 1945 at what, by any standards, has to be considered a ripe old age.

MUSIC TO LET RIP TO

Le Pétomane may have cornered the market as a virtuoso bottom trumpeter, but there are many singers and musicians who have hit the charts with recordings that truly made you want to fart, or that made you think you just had because they stank. Here are the Top Twenty songs about farting that they never actually recorded, but farters everywhere would have rushed out to buy if they'd ever released one.

Pappa Don't Parp	Madonna
C'mon Baby Light My Fart	The Doors
Relight My Fart	Take That (with Lulu)
Wooden Fart	Elvis Presley
Super Pooper	Abba
Please Release Me	Engelbert Whumperstink
You Ain't Smelt Nothing Yet	Bachman-Turner Overdrive
I (Who Have Dropped One)	Shirley Bassey
Wanna Hold Your Breath	Beatles
Rude Vibrations	Beach Boys

Rupture	Blondie
It's A Sin	Pet Shop Boys
My Poo-Pa-Choo	Alvin Stardust
Riftin' All Over The World	Status Quo
I Just Called To Say I Dropped One	Stevie Wonder
Morning Wind Has Broken	Cat Stevens
I Smelt You Babe	Sonny and Cher
Chuff Reaction	Diana Ross
Careless Whumper	George Michael
Bohemian Raspberry	Queen

FARTING TYPES

THE TRICKSTER
One who cons you into participating in his farting escapades.

THE AMBITIOUS GUFFER
One who's always in there first with a fart and quick to sniff out the competition.

THE DUVET SNIFFER
One who farts in bed and puts his head under the duvet to savour the smell.

Go on - pull my finger!

THE TRAMPOLINIST
One who farts in bed and spends the rest of the night bouncing on the mattress trying to get his duvet down off the ceiling.

THE VAMPIRE
One who only farts in the dark and shows his teeth while he's at it.

THE JACUZZI GUFFER
One who farts in the bath to make bubbles.

THE ATHLETE
One who farts while running – applies especially to pole vaulters.

It's not a proper bath without a few bubbles!

THE MUSICIAN
One who amuses his friends with simple tunes.

THE CONNOISSEUR
One who savours his own whiff but can also tell the age, sex and nationality of the perpetrator of any other parp.

THE PATRIOT
One who stands to attention and farts to the tune of
God Save The Queen.

THE NOSY PARKER
One who insists on sticking his nose into other people's
farts.

THE FOOL
One who holds it in for hours and hours, running the
severe risk of follow-through when he finally lets go.

THE ENVIRONMENTALIST
One who worries that his farts are depleting the Ozone
Layer, so does it in his bedroom cupboard.

THE COMEDIAN
One who farts loudly and calls out 'I say, I say, I say! Did you
here the one about two seconds ago?'

THE DEVIL-MAY-CARE
One who farts in board meetings, in lifts, during concerts and even at church.

THE LAZYBONES
One who guffs in the slumped position.

THE GIGGLER
One who lets rip and sniggers.

THE JUDAS
One who denies his own but gives you away when you let off.

THE GEORGE WASHINGTON
One who cannot tell a lie about it.

THE WILLIAM TELL
One who can shoot an apple off your head at ten paces.

The Houdini
One who manages to let a guff escape without anyone knowing when or how.

The Mick Jagger
One who farts into a microphone and yells 'Honky Tonk Woman!'

The Nudist
One who prefers clothing-optional farting and sends up sand-swirls on the beach.

The Wimp
One who jumps at the sound of his own fart.

The Incompetent
One who desperately wants to fart well but usually ends up shitting himself.

The Incontinent
See above.

THE XENOPHOBE
One who hates foreign farts.

THE BUS DRIVER
Well, they all do it constantly . . .

THE MONA LISA
One who farts with an
enigmatic smile.

THE INVOLUNTARY FART

The accidental or involuntary fart is a phenomenon that many will doubtless regard as embarrassing, shocking or even a downright disgrace. For an elderly lady taking that high step up onto the bus or struggling out of an overstuffed armchair after having tea with those nice Jehovah's Witness boys who keep calling round, a loud involuntary fart is understandably unwelcome, although it might discourage the God Squad from making such frequent visits.

For sportspeople, too, the involuntary can be something of a distraction. Long jumpers, high jumpers and pole vaulters are hardly going to put in a personal best (even with the extra wind assistance) if they accidentally let one go at the wrong moment. Neither is it a boost to their confidence to look round and find the umpires and adjudicators falling about laughing. No top gymnast would ever rely on the protein-packed energy locked up in a tin of beans the night before they go swinging their legs around on the pommel horse. The TV crews' microphones pick up even the tiniest sound and, unless you want to broadcast a rectum recital to the nation, you have to take all precautions.

The problem is that when you are concentrating all your physical effort on something other than squeezing out a quick squeaker, it's all too easy for a devilish fart to take your bottom into its own hands, so to speak. This momentary loss of control can induce two vastly different reactions in the experienced, enthusiastic farter – either pleasant surprise or extreme disappointment at having missed the opportunity fully to savour the moment.

The answer is to remain fully in control of your bodily functions, but this is not always going to be possible – just ask any bungee jumper. The involuntary is, therefore, something we all just have to live with. If it is a problem you feel you need to conceal in a domestic situation, buy a leather sofa to disguise the noise and get a dog to take the rest of the blame.

FAMOUS PEOPLE WHO HAVE FARTED

Stalin	The Pope
Batman (and Robin)	The Queen
Victoria Beckham	Ghandi
Hitler	Doris Day
Abraham Lincoln	Mother Theresa
Roy Rogers (and Trigger)	Neil Armstrong
Princess Diana	Genghis Khan
Rob Roy	Michael Schumacher
Al Capone	Florence Nightingale
Lassie	Elvis

PARPING POETRY –
POOR OLD LADY

There was an old lady from Crewe
Who was constantly stricken with 'flu.
She'd cough herself hoarse
And sneeze with such force,
That she'd often let off a few, too!

'Phwoarrr! Was that him or his horse?'

FARTING IN THE MOVIES

There are various fine examples of farting in the movies, and we're talking about on-screen rippers here, not guffing in the cinema, which can make you very unpopular with fellow filmgoers. Obviously two-and-a-half-hours of *Lord of the Rings* with two litres of Pepsi and a bucket of popcorn are going to have an effect, however, so perhaps cinema managers should consider reserving a section of the auditorium for those who enjoy a moving experience along with their movie experience.

On-screen, on the other hand, there are three truly outstanding performances to be appreciated. One is supplied by the inimitable Peter Sellers as Inspector Clouseau in the 1978 movie *Revenge of the Pink Panther*. Cunningly disguised as a mafia don, Clouseau unexpectedly drops one in a crowded elevator. Hilarious when seen in context, the scene is even funnier when you see the entire cast collapse with laughter in the out-takes.

Top of the poops for many, however, is undoubtedly the campfire scene in Mel Brooks' classic 1974 comedy *Blazing Saddles*. This surely holds the all-time record for the most farts delivered in a single movie scene with at least 22 let rip in a 50 second sequence. The farts were accompanied by a windsome volley of belches. Well, what can you expect when you gather together a gang of cowboy outlaws and feed them coffee and beans?

'Who ate all the beans?'

The Blazing Saddles bombardment can only be topped by Jim Carey's virtuoso performance as Lloyd Christmas in the 1994 movie *Dumb & Dumber*. In a dream sequence, Lloyd imagines impressing some sophisticated new friends at a ski-lodge drinks party by lolling back on the sofa, sticking his knees in his ears, blowing off a thunderclap loud enough to cause and avalanche . . . and lighting it! Full marks for style, but Lloyd was almost outdone by his sidekick in the movie, Harry (played by Jeff Daniels), who produced some excruciatingly painful squeaks, toots, rasps and blasts in one of the funniest toilet scenes ever filmed. Unfortunately, having secretly been fed an extra-strong laxative, he was following through, so his efforts can't count.

TOP TWENTY FART FILM TITLES

Here are the Top Twenty Films which, if they were not about farting or didn't even include the merest squeaker, have titles that suggest they really should have done.

Gone With The Wind (1939)

Titanic (1997)

Grease (1978)

Armageddon (1998)

Outbreak (1995)

One Flew Over The Cuckoo's Nest (1976)

Unforgiven (1992)

High Noon (1952)

The Terminator (1984)

Lethal Weapon (1987)

True Grit (1969)

As Good As It Gets (1997)

Howard's End (1992)

Scent Of A Woman (1992)

Misery (1990)

American Beauty (1999)

Lord Of The Rings (2001)

Eyes Wide Shut (1999)

It Could Happen To You (1994)

Days Of Thunder (1990)

'My favourite movie?
Scent Of A Woman, of course!'

TOP TWENTY FART FILMS NEVER MADE

Here are the Top Twenty Fart Films that were never actually made, but should have been.

Carry On Farting

The Postman Always Farts Twice

The Spy Who Dropped One

'It's true –
I always
fart
twice!'

Natural Bum Killers

Shitless In Seattle

You Got Wind

Bravefart

Some Like It Wet

The Godfarter

Incontinence Day

Forrest Whump

The Fartrix

Try Hard

Try Hard With A Vengeance

Pulp Friction

Gutsbusters

Dances With Haemorrhoids

Raging Bum

M'arse Attacks

Peggy Sue Got Gassed

'Darling, you fart divinely ...'

WORDS OF WISDOM

Quando il malato scoppia, il medico piange!

(When a sick man farts, the doctor cries –
Italian saying similar to 'An apple a day keeps
the doctor away.')

PARPING POETRY –
THE ROYAL RIFT

The Queen stomped off in a huff
When Prince Philip let rip a guff
But what he never knew
Was that he'd followed through
And the corgis were covered in the stuff

THE FLATULENCE ADDICTS

For most people, letting rip a satisfying fart once in a while, perhaps in the privacy of your own bathroom or when you're alone in the car, is a pleasant enough experience. Some, however, become seriously addicted to the pleasures of the parp and find themselves having to seek help to control what has become fundamentally anti-social behaviour. Once they have recognised and admitted that they have a problem, the next step is to contact Fartaholics Anonymous.

Fartaholics meetings take place up and down the country at venues that range from Church Halls to the homes of recovering farters.

An addict's first meeting will start with him standing to face his dozen

Would you mind awfully if I didn't come to your meeting, sweeheart?

or so fellow addicts who sit on the floor, cross-legged. The newcomer, let us, for example, call him Dave, because that was his name, then announces to the gathering, 'My name is Dave and I'm a farter.' He then lifts his left leg and lets one rip. The rest of the group then sway from one butt-cheek to another chanting, 'We are with you, Dave. Let it out. Let it out,' guffing as they rock. The trained counsellor at the meeting will then solemnly rise and open a window.

I think I caught that cab just after Dave!

Like many others before him, Dave went on to describe how his farting became a problem that affected his whole life. He was addicted to farting with malice. He was the one who, just as he was paying his cab fare, dropped a real rip-snorter and left it percolating in the back of the taxi for the benefit of the next passenger. He was the one who popped into the elevator on the ground floor, squeezed out a stinker and sent it up to the ninth floor on its own as a little surprise for the next person into the lift. In nightclubs he even took to farting secretly in his girlfriend's handbag and sealing it in as a treat for her when she went to re-do her make-up in the ladies.

The assembled gathering listened silently, with just the occasional hisser or squeaker, and when he had finished they all pissed themselves laughing and fell about farting for all they were worth, striking matches for some celebratory fireworks.

This is the sole purpose of Fartaholics meetings. Let it out, let it out, and have a rollicking good time about it. Exorcise your demons in the company of like-minded rifters and then try to go back to normal life as clenchy-buttocked as everyone else. If more farters attended such meetings, perhaps we could all breathe a little easier.

THE DANGERS OF FARTING

Farting is not, in itself, a dangerous pastime and is actually quite hygienic. Guffs do not carry germs because the environment of the colon is acidic and any bacteria that do get through are harmless. You cannot, therefore, be gassed by a fart unless you happen to be sitting inside a

'Is it plane? Is it a fart . . . ?

bin liner parping away to savour the smell, in which case you will very quickly use up any oxygen emitted with your farts and suffocate. Sitting inside a bin liner, of course, will suffocate you anyway, so it's a particularly stupid thing to do and you shouldn't try it under any circumstances. If you want to enjoy your farts in an enclosed environment, a small room is better, but even the most perverted farting masochist will eventually decide at least to open a window.

While the humble fart holds no inherent danger, the act of farting can be quite hazardous depending on your circumstances. If you happen to be walking a tightrope across Niagara Falls and raise a leg to let one go, you might well come a cropper. Similarly, shifting from one buttock to another to blast off on a ski lift can set up a swaying motion that is dangerous not only to yourself but to everyone else on the lift. Obviously, there is also the risk of setting off an avalanche and, in any case, farting inside a one-piece ski suit is not recommended as you are storing up a nasty surprise for when you unzip it at the end of the day.

Another problem that arises with the bin liner or small room situation is inhaling too much guff gas over a prolonged period. This can poison your system causing light-headedness, headaches and dizzy spells that are highly dangerous to the drivers of bulldozers or tractors with enclosed cabs and anyone who happens to be in the vicinity when such vehicles spin of control due to the driver passing out.

Storing up your farts for an evening of flatulence in front of the TV is also a bad idea. This can be dangerous because trapped wind can cause bloating and abdominal pain and, if you hold on to your guff for too long, it can poison your system making you extremely unwell. So let it all out to be on the safe side.

Letting rip near an open flame is clearly a dangerous thing to do and lighting your farts is simply not a good idea. The flame from a lit guff can shoot out up to a metre and even expert farters have little directional control. The aroma of the fart is also lost, although it is generally replaced by the pungent smell of singed pubes and roasted nuts. The well-documented case of a Danish hospital patient who was undergoing surgery in 1980 illustrates how dangerous an exploding fart can be. The surgeon operating on him was using an electrical surgical knife, much favoured by modern surgeons as they cauterize small blood vessels as they go, preventing unwanted bleeding. Unfortunately, the knife ignited a pocket of intestinal gas, causing an explosion that rippled its way through the poor man's digestive organs. Despite the best efforts of the surgical team to repair the damage, the patient sadly died.

Despite all of these dire warnings, people will continue to fart. We have little choice in the matter. If, however, you feel you want to reduce the risk of dangerous farting as you are, for example, due to walk that tightrope over Niagara Falls in the near future, there are a number of steps you can take to limit your flatulence:

Do avoid spicy foods and those listed in this book as being good for farting.

Don't try out any of the recipes in this book.

Do chew your food properly.

Don't decide to become a vegetarian.

Do remember not to talk while eating.

Don't exercise directly after a meal.

Never wear white underpants.

'It was her in the cable car, wasn't it?'

PARPING POETRY – Devon Delights

There was an old geezer from Devon
Who'd fart on the stroke of eleven.
With baked beans for brunch
And poached eggs for lunch,
He'd be parping till quarter-past seven!

TYPES OF FART

There are only two kinds of farts:
1) Your own
2) Someone else's

ATOMIC FART: The atomic fart is incredibly loud and smells awful, too. It also results in a big explosion, causing everyone to fall to the ground, suffering the effects of methane poisoning.

BABLER BAZOOKA FART (or the Redhill Ripper): The sort of fart that will wake you up at night because it smells so bad! They can be silent or noisy, but they are the most fetid, repulsive, smelliest farts imaginable. In Transylvania, legend has it that even the undead are repulsed by these. They're mostly dropped by women who try to keep them in, but it would be far better for all of us if they let rip frequently.

CHURCH FART: Picture the scene: you're sitting in church, you bend over to pick up a hymn book, and ...'PBBBBBBT'... a giant fart rips out. Fate dictates that you are sitting next to an old lady, who will stare down the pew, looking disgusted.

DELAYED-REACTION FART: You have the urge, but it goes away. You go on about your business and a few seconds, or longer, later, 'BBRRMMPHH'....

EBOLA FART: You are out with some of your friends. One of them farts and before you know it, farting breaks out everywhere.

FOLLOW-THROUGH FART: As Atomic fart, only this time the issuer does not have enough time to get to the bathroom.

GREEN-LIGHT FART: A fart where the conditions make it perfect for it to be released. This one can be as long and loud as the issuer can make it. It rarely occurs in lifts, cars, boardrooms or public places.

HAY FEVER FART: Basically, you fart when you sneeze, but the catch is that you can't smell it.

IRREPRESSIBLE INTERNAL FART: When you try to hold a fart in for too long, the Internal Fart can be worse than the real thing (for you, not bystanders). It often sounds like heavy stomach growling. Not a true fart, but everyone knows that you will have to let it go soon. This fart will always make its way out eventually.

JAPANESE FART: In Japan, it is quite permissible to let rip at the dinner table. So imagine, if you will, a family well satisfied after a fart-inducing meal, openly breaking wind together, unashamedly and with gusto!

KWEEEEEF FART: You are sitting in an orchestra with perfect posture when you let out a fart that sounds like a squeaking clarinet. Being in this musical environment, you can get away with such an emission.

LORD-OF-THE-DANCE FART: In an attempt to cover up the sound of a fart, you switch the topic of conversation to Lord of the Dance and start to stamp your feet loudly on the ground. Whilst you are doing this, you let one escape without anyone noticing.

MORNING FART: The 'first-thing-out-of-bed' fart. Long, loud and not too smelly; very satisfying to release all that gas after the night-time build-up.

MOURNING FART: The fart that lacks research as it has not been definitely proven that anyone has yet died of a fart. Could be applied to anyone disrespectful enough to fart at someone's funeral or on their grave.

NINJA FART: A Ninja is a Japanese warrior trained in ninjutsu, the art of stealth or invisibility. A fart of the same name, therefore, describes a silent emission with a deadly odour.

ORGANIC FART: The person who farts an Organic Fart is usually heavily into health foods and may even ask if you noticed how good, pure and healthy his fart smells. It may smell to you like any other fart, but there is no harm in agreeing with him. He is doing what he thinks is best.

PALMER FART: For years a guy I worked with used to walk into my office, drop one, then depart, shutting my door behind him. I would like his actions to be officially recognised and hereby enter him on to my list of farts. You know who you are!

QUESTIONING FART: This fart starts out low, and rises in pitch towards its conclusion, sounding as if your arse is asking a question.

RED-LIGHT FART: The fart that builds up but never happens alone. Hopefully identified by the issuer and held back.

SADDAM HUSSEIN FART (also known as 'the mother of all farts'): Chemical warfare has begun. You should ring up CNN and send for United Nations inspectors owing to the huge scale of the potential outbreak.

TITANIC FART: This was the really huge fart you did when you were living with your parents. Even now you are grown up they keep reliving it to everyone you introduce them to.

You start to think they might be going to sell the movie rights, and fantasize that Celine Dion will sing the theme song, 'My Fart Will Go On'.

UNDERWATER FART: Often done in the bath, or while swimming. It bears an uncanny resemblance to the sound made by the engine of a nuclear submarine. Can be smelt on rising to the surface, and experienced windbreakers will often catch the fart in an upturned jam-jar, in order to set light to it.

VIAGRA FART: After a long slow fart, you feel yourself aroused.

WEDDING FART: This fart occurs when the vicar pronounces the happy couple husband and wife. An eggy and beefy combination, as well as loud and deadly; when these are on the loose, the bride and groom are the last ones out of the church.

X-RATED FART: This is a fart of such horrifically smelly and sonorific proportions that it must never be allowed to escape in company; essentially a fart that must be emitted in complete privacy.

YOGIC FART: An inevitable by-product of athletic yogic positions and intense concentration. As both the mind and body are focused on supreme relaxation and control, one's ability to monitor the passage of internal gases becomes impaired, and the inevitable occurs.

ZIGZAGGER FART: A particularly tricky and quite crafty emission, it never follows an obvious path. Rather it weaves and winds, meandering with purpose, making it impossible to know with certainty the true origins of the offending fart, and indeed to predict where the fart will come to rest.

FARTING ETIQUETTE

THE RULES

When I am out and about, many people, when hearing my name, ask me about farting etiquette. When, and when not to drop one is a major problem that all of us at some time or other have to face up to. The most common concern and the question I am most frequently asked is, 'I have just started going out with someone and I want to know when is the best time to introduce flatulence into the relationship?'

Let's face it, readers, we have all faced this problem at one time or another! Let me give you an example, and ladies, pardon me for giving this from the male perspective.

You have been dating a very refined lady for a few weeks. You have been out on the town a few times and have eaten at the best establishments your budget allows.

There is one thing that is gnawing away at you and that is having to hold in the build-up of gas for fear of upsetting your date.

Some people I know start as they mean to go on and let rip from day one of a new relationship. I personally find this behaviour loutish and uncouth.

Farting has to be carefully introduced into a relationship to allow both parties the freedom to express themselves. I have listed some of the rules on etiquette to help readers through this social minefield.

'I think I'm ready to fart now, John'.

• By about the fourth date you should now be relaxed in the company of each other. You now feel that the time is right to allow your partner to share with you what up till now has been held back for fear of rejection. Do not, reader, be tempted to let one rocket out which rattles the doors. From past experience I feel that the best way (and here you have to use some skill) is to let a delicate flower of a fart escape your cheeks. It must be loud enough for your date to hear. Now, here is the clever bit. Do not boast or show any pride in your fart, rather show horror and shame. At this point your partner will throw his/her arms around you and tell you not to worry. The ice is broken and both of you can now fart together with ease.

• Never fart near a fresh-food counter – not even an organic-food one. I was once in a supermarket by the fresh-meat counter. Some villain had just unloaded a motherload of putrid pong. A lady nearby was heard to exclaim, 'Do not buy their meat, it has obviously gone off.'

• Ladies, read the above and remember I have written this from a male point of view. The rule for a woman is, whatever you do, do not fart on a first date! Please – and I know this is sexist – let the man do it first. If you do thunder one out, his poor masculinity will be brought into question and the relationship will be doomed. The only exception to this rule is if you are a policewoman or a prison warden. In that case, we males expect it!

• At this point I should bring up the subject of fanny farts. If the affair has already reached the point of freefall farting, then no problem! However, if it has not this may come as a great shock to some men. Ladies, fart warily and do try not to surprise him too soon. Men, should an involuntary rasp occur during lovemaking, be a man and neither recoil in horror – NOR laugh. Be sensitive to how your partner may be feeling and either ignore the parp or reassure your loved one. This way you can laugh long and loud about it with your mates for years to come. I have written a book on this very delicate subject called *Fanny*

Farts – Myth or Just Damn Rude? for those that would like to know more on the subject.

• Lifts and enclosed spaces are a definite no-no. You might like the odour of your farts but others will not.

• Never fart and then embrace your lover whilst wearing an overcoat on a cold day. As we know, hot air rises and your stench will travel upwards and emanate from beneath your coat lapels. Your embrace will be very short as the noxious substance hits your loved one's nostrils.

• Farting in bed (blanket ripping) and then pulling back the covers and sniffing one's own fart is a perfectly acceptable practice. However, pushing your loved one's head under (or Dutch-ovening) must rank as a crime against humanity! This is a very common male habit and I cannot stress enough that it is very unpleasant for the victim – I was once subjected to it by a policewoman.

• Never fart in the company of your mother-in-law/ father-in-law.

• At work, never go into someone's office, drop one and then leave. This was done to me on numerous occasions by a certain gentleman. The odour would linger so much that people coming in an hour later would exclaim, 'Martin's in today then!'

'… and if you fart in the board room again, you're fired!'

• If you are the sole occupant of a bath then farting is to be encouraged as it is a cheap way of enjoying a jacuzzi. However, farting in a bath whilst sharing it is to be discouraged. The effect of the hot water on the lower intestines is such that you could end up firing out a gust of gas and worse. There is nothing more embarrassing than sharing your bath with your partner and something nasty.

• My last rule is the most important. You must take heed of this even if you ignore all my other rules. After six pints of beer and a chicken curry do not go to work wearing light-coloured trousers. I am sure I do not need to spell it out for you. Your whole career could rest on keeping to this rule with complete fidelity.

PARPING POETRY – The Sailor

There is a young yachtsman from Wales,
Whose boating technique never fails.
He dines on baked beans
And plenty of greens,
So his farts put the wind in his sails.

CLASSIC FART JOKES

I couldn't resist lowering the tone of this book by sharing some of my favourite farting jokes of all time - and, just like a fart, the best ones hang around the longest. Honk as loud as you like!

How can you tell if a woman is wearing tights?
If she farts her ankles blow up.

Her marriage into high society was an excuse for Lady Bountiful to entertain lavishly. Unfortunately, she was unused to all the rich food and soon found that she was permanently bloated and full of wind. Her embarrassment was complete when, during a banquet for a visiting diplomat, she let go a corker. So she blamed it on the butler who was standing behind her, crying loud enough for everyone in the room to hear, 'Jeeves, stop that!' To which Jeeves replied, 'Certainly, madam, which way did it go?'

Three guys were on a plane. The first guy said, 'I'll drop this knife and see where it lands.' The second guy said, 'I'll drop this gun and see where it lands.' The third guy says, 'I'll drop this petrol bomb and see where it lands.' Then they all jump out of the plane and parachute down to see what the results are. The first guy sees this kid crying. He says, 'Hey, kid, why are you crying?' The kid explains that he has just got hit on the head by a knife. The second guy also finds a kid in tears and it turns out the kid got hit in the head by a gun. The third guy, however, finds a kid rolling on the ground, laughing. 'Hey, kid,' he says. 'What's so funny?' The kid replies, 'I just farted and that building blew up!'

Why do farts smell?
So deaf people can enjoy them too.

Stepping into the elevator the businessman quickly detected an offensive odour. The only other occupant was a little old lady. 'Excuse me,' he addressed her, 'did you happen to break wind?' 'Of course I did,' she replied. 'You don't think I stink like this all the time, do you?'

Ab Mustafa was in the Arab bazaar one day when he felt a terrible pain in his stomach. He couldn't control the thunderous fart which followed. It boomed above the general hubbub and all around him were staggered. Ab Mustafa was so embarrassed that he ran home, packed his bags and left town. He didn't return for twenty years. Then, thinking it safe, he came back to find the bazaar much changed and modernized. At a carpet stall he asked a young boy who had built the new camel stables at the far end of the bazaar, and the young boy replied: 'Oh, that was built fourteen years and three days after Ab Mustafa farted in the bazaar and left town.'

A guy walks into a bar and bets the bartender £20 that he can fart the national anthem. When the bartender agrees, the dude jumps up on the bar, squats, drops his pants and shits all over the bar. The bartender goes nuts and yells 'What the hell are you doing?' The farter explains, 'Hey, even Pavarotti has to clear his throat before a performance!'

A rather sad young man was still a virgin as he approached the ripe old age of thirty. So his mates lined him up with a willing and voracious young lady for his birthday present. Cheered on by his mates, the birthday boy had no choice but to go off with the woman. At first she stuck to basics but then she manoeuvred them into the soixante-neuf position. Unfortunately, she suddenly felt a rumble and let go a fart. The birthday boy got the full blast and threw her off him saying: 'Christ, what the hell is soixante-dix then?' Unfortunately for his mates, he is still a virgin.

A Red Indian chief has a problem passing wind so he sends son Number 1 to the doctor. The son arrives at the doctor's and says 'Big Chief No Fart'. The doctor gives son Number 1 some fart pills but he returns the next day and says 'Big Chief No Fart' and the following day 'Big Chief Still No Fart'. Eventually the doctor gives him the strongest laxatives he has in his possession and tells son Number 1 to give these to his father. The next day the doctor hears a wailing at the Indian camp and sets out to discover what is amiss. He sees son Number 1 being decked out in war paint and feathers. 'What news?' he asks him. The son replies, 'Big Fart No Chief'.

What is the definition of a fart?
A turd honking for the right of way.

What do you get when you've been eating onions and beans?
Tear gas.

A man went into the doctor's and confessed to an embarrassing problem. 'I fart all the time, Doctor. But they are soundless and they are odourless. In fact, since I've been here, I've farted no less than five times. What do I do about it?' 'Here's a prescription, Mr Brown,' said the doctor. 'Take these pills three times daily for a week and then come back and see me.' The following week, a disappointed Mr Brown arrived at the surgery. 'Doctor, I'm farting as much as ever, but now they smell terrible as well.' 'Mr Brown,' said the doctor, 'think yourself a lucky man. Now that we've fixed your sinuses, we'll fix your hearing.'

What is green and smells?
Hulk's fart.

In the geriatric ward, old Ben was dozing in his chair. Every time he leaned to one side a nurse would gently push him straight. A new patient arrived and asked how he found being in the ward: 'Oh it's all right,' said old Ben. 'But that young nurse makes it bloody difficult for one to have a fart.'

'I always find that when farting in polite company, a simple hand gesture distracts people's attention.'

The Queen was showing the Archbishop of Canterbury around her new stables when a stallion nearby let go such a resounding fart it rattled the windows and couldn't be ignored.

'Oh dear,' said the Queen, blushing, 'I'm frightfully sorry about that.'

'Think nothing of it, Ma'am,' said the archbishop. 'All actions are God-given. But anyway, I thought it was the stallion.'

A girl really fancied a man. So when he asked her out for a date she was delighted. However, on the day of days she had a tummy bug. She couldn't bear to call the date off so she ate a lot of stomach-calming herbal tablets and waited for them to take effect. When he arrived, she dashed out of the flat giving him no time to come inside and smell the farty odour there. She got into his car and, as he waited for the traffic to ease up until he could open the driver's door, she thought she'd just risk letting a small one go. It was quite loud although thankfully not a stinker and she was just starting to relax when she heard a cough from behind her: 'Excuse me, dear, but may we introduce ourselves? We are John's parents.'

A fart: a belch that didn't find the lift.
A belch: a fart that caught the lift.

A wealthy playboy met a beautiful young girl in an exclusive lounge. He took her to his lavish apartment where he soon discovered she was not a tramp, but was well-groomed and very intelligent. Hoping to get her into bed he began to show her his collection of priceless antiques and paintings, and he offered her a glass of champagne. 'Oh I'd love a glass,' she replied. 'It is the most romantic, sexy drink on earth and just looking at an uncorked bottle fills me with the greatest excitement and anticipation. When the bubbles go up my nose, I am transported to a seventh heaven, and once I've finished the bottle I am so horny I am just about anybody's. On the other hand, I'll pass. All those bubbles make me fart.'

A woman who loved baked beans had to give them up because they caused her to fart too much. However, it was her birthday, and after having a few drinks at the office after work her resistance was lowered, so that she went into the fish-and-chip shop on the way home and ordered some pots of piping-hot baked beans. She figured that if she walked all the way home afterwards she could blow most of the effects out safely by the time she got there. Thus she set off at a brisk pace and soon began farting loudly.

Her husband met her at the door of her house, seeming worried that she was so much later than usual. 'Hurry up,' he said impatiently, 'I have a surprise for you.' Before he would let her over the threshold, he insisted that he blindfold her, and then he led her into the dining-room. 'Just wait here one minute,' he said, 'I'll be back in a tick.' As she sat waiting, she felt a burning sensation in her bottom and knew she had to let one go. So, taking advantage of the fact that her husband was out of the room, she parped away - at least five escaping in quick succession. Another minute passed and she farted a few more times until she heard her husband's footsteps returning. 'Happy birthday, darling,' he cried, removing her blindfold, and there sat six of her friends.

A guy comes home from the pub, rolling drunk, and falls into bed. His wife is asleep and he is glad that he hasn't woken her. He also feels free to let off a beer fart. The fart is loud and long and very, very smelly so that even its creator starts to choke. The wife also wakes up and says, 'What the hell was that?'

'Um … goal! One-Nil! GOAL!' replies the husband.

'You drunk bastard,' thinks the wife and squeezing her buttocks together tightly manages to fart herself. 'One-All!' she snarls and rolls over and goes back to sleep.

'You smug cow,' thinks the husband, somewhat riled. He takes a few deep breaths, sucks in his stomach and … shits in the bed.

He reflects on his situation for a moment and then nudges his wife in the back: 'Oi, wake up. Half time, switch sides.'

A Japanese and an American are playing golf. The Japanese man gets ready to tee off but before he actually does so he sticks his thumb in front of his mouth and appears to be talking to it. The American says, 'What are you doing?' The Japanese replies, 'Oh, don't worry. I have a minute phone device inserted in my thumb and I was sending a message.'

They continue to play golf and all of a sudden the American makes a noise that sounds like a fart. The Japanese looks over at him questioningly. 'Oh, says the American. Don't worry. I was just getting a message.'

An air-freshener seller gets into a lift where she is overcome by a rumbly tummy and lets go a shocker of a fart. 'Ah ha!' she thinks, 'no worries,' and takes out one of her samples of pine air-freshener and gives it a liberal spray.

At the next floor a man gets in. 'Christ,' he says, 'What's that smell?'

The lady replies: 'Oh, that's my pine air freshener.'

'Pine air freshener?' chokes the man. 'It smells more like someone shat on a Christmas tree.'

A guy is invited to dinner by his new girlfriend's parents. He is sitting at the table and their pet dog keeps biting at his ankles. He bends over to stop it and accidentally lets slip a fart. The girl's mother promptly cries, 'Rover, stop it, come away!' The guy is relieved and when another fart builds up, he just lets that one off too.

'Rover, PLEASE come away,' shouts the mother. The young man is now feeling safe enough to let go a third which rumbles loudly out of his backside. He looks at the dog accusingly and the girl's mother screams, 'Rover, come away now, before he shits on you.'

There was an old married couple who had lived together for nearly forty years. The only problem in their relationship was the husband's bad habit of breaking wind every morning – setting off his own dawn chorus. The wife was in despair and on their forty-first anniversary she awoke as usual with watering eyes and gasping for breath. Enough was enough, she decided. Up she got and went downstairs into the kitchen where she mixed together in a bowl mashed potatoes, gravy, uncooked liver, a haggis and red wine. Then she crept back upstairs with her bowl and, checking that her husband was indeed still asleep, and was indeed still farting away, she emptied the contents into the bed beside him.

An hour later she heard her husband wake up and then a couple of huge farts reverberate off the floorboards above her head. This was soon followed by a blood-curdling scream and the sound of frantic scurrying about upstairs. The wife could not control herself and burst out laughing, so much so that she had to put a tea-towel in her mouth to stop the guffaws. She had finally got her revenge.

Her husband appeared about half an hour later with the 'blood-stained' sheet and his pyjamas in his hand. He was very white and strangely quiet. He said 'Wife, you were right – all those years that I didn't listen to you and now I know I should have listened harder.'

'What do you mean?' asked the wife, trying to look innocent.

'Well you always told me that I would end up farting my guts out one of these days, and this morning it finally happened. But by the grace of God and these two fingers, I think I got them all back in.'

Q: What's the definition of a surprise?
A: A fart with a lump in it.

WORDS OF WISDOM

Serve the Germans with all your heart;
Your reward will be a fart.

POLISH SAYING

Vegetarianism is harmless enough, though it is
apt to fill a man with wind and self-
righteousness.

SIR ROBERT HUTCHINSON

FARTING FACTS

There are very few resources available for Guffologists to research facts about farting, but over the years, through extensive personal experience and reliable reports from eye-witnesses, I have managed to fill a whole filing cabinet with fart information. There follows a selection of the most interesting extracts from my files.

Most people pass somewhere between 200 and 2,00 ml of guff gas each day.

A healthy male will normally let off between ten and twenty times a day.

It has been reported that a man in Oklahoma (living in the place not appearing in the musical) farted as often as 145 times a day, including 83 guffs in one four-hour period.

Women fart less than men with only eight or nine parps a day, but they still deny it.

The average man releases enough guff each day to inflate a small balloon.

Women may fart less than men but theirs sound as loud and smell just as bad.

Like all good perfumes, after about two minutes our noses can no longer detect the odour of a fart.

Farting in a bottle and sticking the cork in will preserve your guff – the smell that is, not the sound.

Precautions must be taken when measuring sustained male emissions.

Farts will generally only hang around for two to five minutes before they are dispersed in the air of a room.

A fart can travel up to 15 metres depending on wind conditions or air circulation in a room.

More than half the gas in a fart is usually Carbon Dioxide.

Carbon Dioxide is heavier than air and helps to keep farts at a low level, rather than letting the lighter fart gases take them up to the ceiling.

Farting makes a noise due to the vibration the parp causes when the internal pressure sends it rocketing through your ringpiece – just like the air coming out of a party balloon.

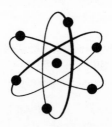

THE FARTING PEASANT

The French, who are masterful farters, have many tales from their history concerning *le guff grande*, one of which dates back to the fourteenth century and is entitled *Le Pet au vilain* (*The Peasant's Fart*). The story has it that a peasant was suffering so terribly from indigestion that the Devil, believing the man was going to die, sent one of his minions to catch the poor man's soul in a sack as he expired. The peasant, however, farted hugely instead, straight into the sack. Thinking to have trapped another soul, the minion dashed back to Hell with his prize. On opening the sack, however, the Devil was hit by a whiff that made even the stinking pits of Hell smell like pot-pourri on God's mantelpiece. Outraged by the stench, the Devil vowed never to accept any souls like it into his domain if they were all going to smell as bad. So, from that day forth, no French peasant has ever gone to Hell.

PROCTOLOGISTS TO THE QUEEN

In more elevated circles, the late Lord Adeane (1910-84), who, as Sir Michael Adeane, was Private Secretary to the Queen from 1953 until his retirement in 1972, was a man famed for his wit as well as for the graceful tact, without which no such courtier can last for long. On one occasion at Buckingham Palace he excused himself to a colleague, saying that he had to take a party of proctologists (specialists in matters affecting the rectum, if you must know) for an audience with the Sovereign.

'What on earth are proctologists?' his friend asked.

'Bottom doctors, my dear chap – bottom doctors,' Adeane replied gaily.

'Good heavens! How ghastly! How on earth will you introduce them to Her Majesty?'

'Simple – I shall say they are fundamentalists.'

'I'm looking up the Queen next week.'

PARPING POETRY –
AN ODE TAE A FERT

Oh what a sleekit horrible beastie
Lurks in yer belly efter the feastie
Just as ye sit doon among yer kin
There sterts to stir an enormous wind

The neeps and tatties and mushy peas
stert workin like a gentle breeze
but soon the puddin wi the sauncie face
will have ye blawin all ower the place

Nae matter whit the hell ye dae
a'bodys gonnae have tae pay
even if ye try to stifle
It's like a bullet oot a rifle

Hawd yer bum tight tae the chair
tae try and stop the leakin air
shify yersel fae cheek tae cheek
Prae tae God it doesnae reek

But aw yer efforts go assunder
oot it comes like a clap a thunder
Ricochets aroon the room
michty me a sonic boom

God almighty it fairly reeks
Hope I huvnae shit ma breeks
tae the bog I better scurry
aw whit the hell, it's no ma worry

A'body roon aboot me chokin
wan or two are nearly bokin
I'll feel better for a while
Cannae help but raise a smile

Wis him! I shout with accusin glower
alas too late, he's just keeled ower
Ye dirty bugger they shout and stare
A dinnae feel welcome any mair

Where e're ye go let yer wind gan' free
sounds like just the job fur me
whit a fuss at Rabbie's perty
ower the sake o' won wee ferty!

ANON.

FAMOUS FART QUOTES

I will not permit thirty men to travel four hundred miles to agitate a bag of wind.
ANDREW DICKSON WHITE, US EDUCATIONALIST

Chevy Chase couldn't ad-lib a fart after a baked bean dinner.
JOHNNY CARSON, US CHAT-SHOW HOST

Gerry Ford is so dumb he can't fart and chew gum at the same time.
LYNDON B. JOHNSON, US PRESIDENT

I have more talent in my smallest fart than you have in your entire body.
WALTER MATTHAU TO BARBARA STREISAND

Acting is largely a matter of farting about in disguises.
PETER O'TOOLE, BRITISH ACTOR

THE GUFF SPECTROMETER

You can't see a fart. You can see where it's been by taking a look at the people in a room who have gone blue in the face or fainted on the floor, but you can't actually see a fart. Farts are invisible, otherwise the SBD (Silent But Deadly) would probably be known as the SBCLAT (Silent But Christ Look At That!). Your local pub would look like every man at the bar was drinking with the ghost of a long-lost friend – and in many ways they are – as clouds of farts wafted around behind them. And there would be no denying that it was you who farted on the bus if there were a brown cloud sitting on the seat beside you. You'd never be able to see the movie on a long-haul flight. The guff, then, is quite an elusive creature. You can, of course, light it, but that is highly dangerous and, since the flames are consuming the substance of the whump, you are seeing neither its shape nor its form. To allow Guffologists to study the formation of a fart, therefore, an apparatus known as the Guff Spectrometer (illustrated opposite) was developed. Sadly, it was never possible to calibrate the Spectrometer to a level sensitive enough to pick up only a little squeaker, so a huge volume of guff gas was required. This had the unfortunate effect either of blurring the vision of the operators so much that they couldn't see a thing, or of making them pass out completely before they caught even a glimpse of a fart. Quite what a fart looks like, then, remains a mystery.

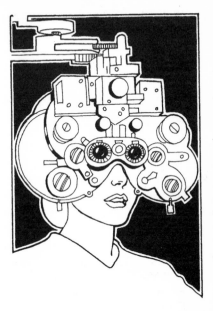

THE STORY OF ABU HASSAN

The story of Abu Hasan appears in Sir Richard Burton's translation of *The Book of the Thousand Nights and a Night*, otherwise known as *The Arabian Nights Entertainments*, and was privately published in 1885. His version is as follows:

Abu Hasan was an opulent merchant. His wife died when both were still young and his friends urged him to marry again. Abu Hasan duly entered into negotiations with a maid of great beauty. The wedding banquet was a great celebration and everyone was invited. 'The whole house was thrown open to feasting: there were rices of five different colours, and sherbets of as many more; and kid goats stuffed with walnuts, almonds and pistachios; and a young camel roasted whole. So they ate and drank and made mirth and merriment; and the bride was displayed in her seven dresses.'

Eventually the bridegroom was summoned to the chamber where his bride sat enthroned, and he rose slowly and with dignity from his divan; but as he did so, 'because he was overfull of meat and drink, lo and behold! he brake wind, great and terrible. Thereupon each guest turned to his neighbour and talked aloud, and made as though he has heard nothing.' Abu Hasan, however, was terribly embarrassed. Instead of going to the bridal chamber he went down to the courtyard, saddled his horse and rode to the harbour, where he boarded a ship about to sail to India. There he remained for ten years, but at the end of that time 'he was seized with homesickness, and the longing to behold his native land was that of a lover pining for his beloved; and he came near to die of yearning desire.' Abu Hasan returned secretly to his native land, disguised in rags. 'But when he drew near his old home, he looked down upon it from the hills with brimming eyes, and said to himself, "There is a chance that they might know thee; so I will wander about the outskirts and hearken to the folk. Allah grant that what happened to me be not remembered by them."'

'He listened carefully for seven nights and seven days, till it so chanced that, as he was sitting at the door of a hut, he heard the voice of a young girl saying. "O my mother, tell me the day when I was born, for one of my companions is about to tell my fortune." And the mother answered, "Thou was born, O my daughter, on the very night when Abu Hasan brake wind.'"

When Abu Hasan heard these words 'he rose up from the bench and fled, saying to himself, "Verily thy breaking of wind hath become a date, which shall last for ever and ever."' He returned to India and remained in exile for the rest of his life.

FUEL OF THE FUTURE?

It has long been accepted that the farts from the huge numbers of cows and sheep in Australia and New Zealand are contributing to the deterioration of the ozone layer above the South Pole. This, of course, could ultimately lead to the melting of the polar ice cap and a watery grave for us all, but the answer not only to the problem with the ozone layer but also to that of the world's energy crisis is at hand!

All we have to do is simply connect large balloons to the bums of all the cows and sheep in the world to collect the methane gas that is harming the ozone layer. The gas will be collected daily, piped into much larger balloons and brought to distribution centres where it will be transferred to zeppelins for shipment around the world. The beauty of the scheme is that the lighter-than-air gas will both send the zeppelins skywards and fuel the gas-powered engines. The world's first self-transporting fuel will soon be powering cars, trains, electricity generators and aircraft.

This will phase out fossil fuel and eliminate the methane which will be consumed by the world's engines.

Studies have shown that there is a danger that, unless primary gas collection is effected on a regular basis, many sheep and some of the smaller cows might float away, causing a danger to air traffic, but this is surely a small price to pay for saving the world.

'Uh-oh . . . I knew I shouldn't have had beans before blast-off!'

PARPING POETRY – The Garden Scent

A gardener hailing from Leeds
Would fart when he stooped to pick weeds.
He'd fluff when he hoed,
Blow off when he mowed
And let rip when he bent to plant seeds.

And suddenly there came a
sound from heaven
as of a rushing mighty wind,
and it filled all the house
where they were sitting.
Acts 2:2

BIBLIOGRAPHY & FURTHER READING

1) *Tailwinds*, Peter Furze, 1998; Michael O' Mara Books, London

2) *The Little Book of Farting*, Alec Bromcie, 1999; Michael O'Mara Books, London

3) *The History of Farting* (worldwide bestseller), Dr Benjamin Bart, 1995; Michael O'Mara Books, London

4) *Thunder, Flush & Thomas Crapper*, Adam Hart-Davis, 1997; Michael O'Mara Books, London

5) *The Little Toilet Book*, compiled by David Brown, 1999; Michael O'Mara Books, London

6) The next edition of this book

7) *Bubbles in the Bath* by Ivor Windybottom

8) Benjamin Franklin wrote a book called *Fart Proudly*. It is hard to find but you might be lucky enough to come across it.

PS! There are also many interesting fartsites on the Web these days for interested browsers.

* Publisher's note: Unfortunately, *Fanny Farts – Myth or Just Damn Rude?* is currently out of print.

PUBLISHER'S DISCLAIMER

Any person who attempts either of the following does so at their own risk: lighting farts or trying out any of I. Dunwun's farting recipes. The first practice is deemed by both the publisher and the author to be a dangerous and infantile pastime, and although there are passing references to it in this book, at no stage is it advocated. It should be noted that the publisher has neither tried nor tested I. Dunwun's recipes, and therefore recommends that participants proceed with extreme caution and that they should reduce some of the ingredients such as curry powder.

While the statistics and factual information in this book have been verified by the publisher wherever possible, all such information was provided by the author. While much of it is proven fact, a great deal is clearly utter gibberish and the reader must judge for himself how much of it he chooses to believe.